It's October 8, 2021, and I am going to change the mood of this book. I am going to add the dreams I've had so far. It's not many dreams, but I feel as if I must rush this book for some strange reason therefore, I will not make this book too long.

Hopefully I will not have more than 40 pages.

Listen, Allelujah.

Have mercy Lovey because the worst is yet to come.

We have to now gather our good and true own.
The Exodus must now begin.

Children and People of God – God's good and true own, please listen to me. <u>*IT'S TIME TO COME HOME.*</u>

<u>*IT'S TIME FOR THE EXODUS.*</u>

<u>*WE NEED TO FIND EACH OTHER AND GATHER IN THE LAND AND LANDS LOVEY NEED US TO BE IN BECAUSE, IT'S MORE THAN CRITICAL TIME NOW.*</u>

<u>*TWO (2) JUDGEMENT IS GOING TO FACE EARTH, AND WE NEED TO BE AWAY FROM THE CHILDREN AND PEOPLE OF DEATH.*</u>

<u>*KNOW:*</u>

God did not put STRIFE BETWEEN THE DEVIL'S SEED AND GOD'S SEED. HUMANS DID THAT ALL BY THEMSELVES.

God cannot put strife in the heart of anyone.

Life – God knoweth not Death therefore, Life and Death are truly different in the truest of sense.

Life will forever ever seek and do all to separate self from Evil.

All that evil do is right for them; evil because, evil people live for Death; a place in Hell; their Hell.

Evil cannot see their wrongs. All that wicked and evil people do, they cannot see their wrongs because to them; their wrongs are right never wrong.

All the evils Wicked and Evil People do unto others, they feel they are justified.

Have mercy God and help me to deliver our children and people to the land and lands you need them to be in.

Dear God, be our lawmaker, guide, truth, governor, path, pathway, hope, water source, food source, health source, financial source, and more Lovey because we; our children and people truly need you right now.

Lovey you have to; need to be our water and true organic fertilizer that help us to grow good and true. Lovey, you are my good and true truth therefore, I am going to give you this song in hope that you will hear me, and turn your light, water, all that is good blessing wise, truth wise, hope wise, and more wise on our good and true home as we journey good and true home to you.

MY GOVERNOR by Luciano feat. Cocoa Tea

When it comes to Black People Lovey, I refuse to fight with anyone of them for their beliefs.

I refuse to be like the Messengers of Old that had problems with Black People. Time and time again you Lovey have and has shown me that Black People will not accept me. They will not listen to me, <u>and this is truly fine with me.</u> <u>I care not if Black People accept me or not. I AM NOT BEGGING FRIENDS, OR BELIEFS.</u> I am here to save the Saved of Life and in Life. If Black People want to continue to go to Hell so be it. Trust me, I am leaving their ignorant and stupid ass behind. I refuse unintelligent People that would rather Death over You; Life Lovey. Trust me, <u>WHEN OUR PEOPLE ARE SAFELY IN THE LAND AND LANDS YOU NEED US TO BE, I AM THE ONE TO LIF UP MI DRESS AND TELL THE REST OF THE BLACK NATION TO KISS MY NATURAL BROWN ASS BECAUSE, I KNOW ALL WHO DO NOT LISTEN IS HELL BOUND DUE TO THEIR OWN STUPIDITY AND IGNORANCE.</u>

No Lovey, let the Bible of Man Judge their ass because I know for a fact without doubt, the Bible of Man is going to Judge their ass. And, so should it be Lovey.

Black People believe in too much nastiness as well as, too accepting of lies; all that is unclean; sinful.

So yes, your Sin and Sins Judge you and now, the Bible of Man will Judge you.

And Lovey, once all is said and done; absolutely no laggers Lovey.

None bout dem neva ready.
None bout dem neva noa.
None bout mi sarry.
None bout dem neva ha enough time.
None bout it's not fair.

All the excuses in the different Books of Blacks will come into play Lovey and truss mi, mi wi lif yu up Lovey an put yu aside an sey, mek mi.

The Loudspeaker would and will turn to full blast, and too late will play for all to hear whilst me saying; "__KISS IT BITCHES.__" __You should have known God would not deceive you, nor would God use Religion and Profits; whoops Prophets to deceive any of you, preach to you, educate you, save you, and more.__

__Knowing God is not lacking trust or knowledge.__

__Knowing God is not sitting on your lazy ass and expect God to do all for you.__

No, I am getting pissed now. God can't be saving your dumb ass, and you are not seeing, and knowing how God is saving you.

The Bible of Man is a Lie – Categorical Sin. Question the damned book – Man's So-called Holy Bible from the beginning to the end.

GOD IS NOT NASTY, HUMANS ARE.

Look how Nasty the White Race has and have made God in their so-called Holy Bible. Nastiness billions believe in and think God is going to save you from the shit you believe in about God.

Well, let me tell all of you this. GOD WILL NOT SAVE YOU.

GOD HAS AND HAVE WALKED AWAY FROM BILLIONS OF YOU. *And if it was not so, I would not tell you this.*

Dyam wrenk. YOU AS HUMANS CANNOT PUT YOUR NASTY AND DIRTY SELF ON THE LEVEL OF GOD BECAUSE, GOD IS NOT ANYONE'S BITCH NOR IS GOD A FLESHY LIKE HUMANS.

Now tell me, why would God lie to humans?
Why would God be a giver backer taker?
Why would God go against his and or, her word?

Why would God give his prophets one set of laws to live by and the rest of the citizens of the land different laws?

Is God that hopeless and incompetent?

Are the Prophets of Men above the Law and God that they have different set of laws to govern them?

So now tell me, are prophets not like your Lying Politicians and Religious Leaders that put themselves above the Law and Laws of God?

Without God all you have left is Death, and many are without life here on Earth therefore, their Spirit must die Spiritually.

No, don't forget the "WAGES (PAY) OF SIN IS DEATH."

IT IS NOT YOUR FLESH THAT PAYS FOR YOUR SINS, IT IS YOUR SPIRIT. *Therefore, billions hath no life in life with Lovey; God.*

The dreams are at the end of the book.

Michelle

In order to know you, you have to know yourself.

Life is a given therefore, make wise choices in life.

It is a foolish person that do not think of their Spiritual Life as life is not Physical alone, it is Spiritual also.

Strive to be the best you you can be because, <u>absolutely no one can live the next person's life for them.</u>

My life is my life. Do not want or need to be me, want and need to be you, the good and true you not the negative you.

It's not all you plant can grow. Some seeds are not true to life they've been genetically modified.

We say life is hard.
Why me Lord?
Why do I have to suffer?
Why did I have to be born?
Those questions are not for God to answer.
Those questions are for your parents to answer.
You to answer.

God did not create your hardships, therefore, look into the life of your parents and ancestors on a whole.

Look into the life you've shaped for you here on Earth.

Life is not just receiving alone. Life is giving as well.

PEOPLE LIKE YOU by Gramps Morgan

Life is good and true.

It is us as humans that take life from us.

It is you as humans that put your life in the hands of demons to destroy you. Demons like your Religious Leaders – Demons, Political Leaders – Demons, Corporate Greed – Demons, and more.

Michelle
September 18, 2021
Edited October 9 – 10, 2021

Come with me.
Take my hand
Dinner for two
Wine
No caviar
Strawberry or Vanilla Ice Cream
Maybe Cherry
You make the choice

By the river
Sea
Our terrace
Upstairs verandah
This I leave up to you too

Smile
You are my mood
Sweat
Fountain of you

Yes, I am bloating your head
But I am right
True to you

You're my bed
Smooth ride
Forever play
Well, mine for all time.

Michelle
September 18, 2021
Edited October 09, 2021

I think I am going crazy but:
Do you truly love the smell of bleach on your white clothes?
Your hand
Bed linen

Wow because lately:
I am into truly whites
Just seeing the true white in my clothes
Yes, exotic for me
Weird for you
Truly sick for some

But:
I am me
You are you
You cannot be me
And, I cannot be you

But wow
Yep
The whacked out me from time to time.

Michelle
September 18, 2021

Oh my gosh
Let me have some fun
Sit with me
Orange for two
Just you and me

No not by the fire
Fireplace
River
Sea

But:
Us in bed
Lying in each other's arms
Listening to each other's heartbeat

Yes, this is our time together
No kids around
Just me and you enjoying each other

No talking
Just eating
Listening
Being at true peace with each other.

Michelle
September 18, 2021

Let me taste your lips
Sweet kiss
Tender caress
Fine wine
Divine

Let me comb your hair
Twist your lox
Wash it too
Be your tender touch

Take me in your arms
Dance with me
Let me look up at you
See the glee in thy smile

Now:
Lower you head and kiss me
Savour me as I savour you

Don't let the evening or night end
Just wrap me in your arms
Hold me tight

Put your legs around mine
Let me fall asleep with you

Aah bliss
Good Morning Sunshine.

Michelle
September 18, 2021

I need true love in a major way
Can you be true to me?
Are you weak?
Strong
Intelligent
Powerful
Power hungry
Controlling

Are you carefree?
Easy going
Tender
A roamer
Loner
Vagabond

Are you stable?
Well educated
Wise
Friendly
Truthful
True to you

And no, I truly do not know where this is going.

Truly think of you
Me too
Do answer
And please, don't ask yourself why?

Michelle
September 18, 2021

Yes, I want to play
Writing in this way for me is fun
Gives me joy
Put a smile on my face

Yes, I am thinking of you
Wondering if you are smiling as I am smiling

Are you enjoying?
Thinking too

Have fun with me
Enjoy me
Enjoy you
You are my fun and play

Take my hand
Squeeze it
Not to hard

Lightly
Do you feel me
Feel my essence
See my smile
Feel my joy

Hey
That's me and you
Be happy
As:
I am truly happy with you.

Michelle
September 18, 2021

Be my grace
Social Media
True Confidant
True friend
True everything

If you agree
We can't hurt each other
We can't love each other
We can't lie to each other ever

No, it's not ooooooh
I don't believe in love
Truly do not know love anymore
Do not want or need love
Truly do not want or need you to love me

Come on
Don't throw the book down
Don't say I have lost you
Stop saying but we are true
Now, let me explain

I do not need or want love from you

I NEED AND WANT YOUR TRUE LOVE

I am not a love person

See
It's the ones that say they love you that:
Hurt you
Cheat on you
Disappoint you
Bring home all kinds of diseases to you
Have the other woman or man with you

Steal from you
Some even kill you
Some control you
Abuse you

You get the picture
See where I am going

So no, I truly do not need or want love
I need and want true love

True Love cannot:
Hurt you
Shame you
Body shame you
Cheat on you
Bring home diseases to you
Lie to you
Die for you

True Love:
Is true respect

True growth physically and spiritually therefore, true love cannot die for you as true love is life, truth growth, and more good and true things.

True Love:
Is warm
Oooh my gosh is true love ever warm

True Love:
Protects
Wow is true love ever protecting

Therefore, true love is me and you.

Never ending
Never dying
Forever ever growing true.

Now, do you see?
Do you get me?
Will you be true to me?
Forever ever protecting me
Growing and building with me good and true

If I need rescuing
Would you rescue me
Comfort me
Hold me
Never let me go

Would you tell me you truly love me?
Are my world of truth and care?

Yes, many questions.
Find me
Tell me you truly love me.

Michelle
September 18, 2021
Edited October 09, 2021

Place your head on my shoulder
Let me take you to dinner
Yes, table for two
You and me
My treat

Don't even think it and say:
I'm the man
I should pay for dinner

Nope, not tonight baby
Tonight, it's me pampering you
Me taking care of you
Me truly loving you
Me appreciating you
Me thanking you for being you

So
Sit back
Relax
Enjoy
Let me do for you good and true.

Michelle
September 18, 2021
Edited October 09, 2021

Okay, okay
You've had a rough day
Boss pissed you off
Is a goof
Jackass
This I know
Keep it outside

You're home
Dinner is ready
Your bath is set
Enjoy

No
You're home
This is not work
Your workplace
So, leave that stress and yes shit
Outside the door

I did not marry your work
Your workplace
Workload
Stress
I married you

Therefore, know the difference between work and home.

Know the difference between your wife and home.
What you are paid for; to do.
What you are paid at work to do.

Home is truly not work.

I am not your workload
Homework

Boss's stress

He or she may take their work home with them but, you leave yours outside the door.

Now, relax
Let me take your briefcase
Now, take my hand
I will lead you up the stairs

Do nothing
Let me take your clothes off
Stop
Relax
It's your bath
Have fun
When you are ready
Just call
I will bring dinner to you

So, unwind and enjoy the ride.

Michelle
September 18, 2021
Edited October 09, 2021

Please forgive me
No, I truly don't care if you don't like me
Truly don't care if you hate me
You can't be me
I have to be me
Live with me and for me

So, continue to hate me
Your hate means absolutely nothing to me
Abey, if yu nuh like me.
Abey, if yu caane stan mi
Abey, if mi life betta dan fi yu
Abey, if Gad truly love mi an nuh love yu or truly love yu
Dutty caane cum clean
An, yu dutty
Mucky
Stink

Not even drangcrow waane pitch pan yu

Cu yu tu
Uglier dan sin

Clear off
Leave me alone

You are not apart of my world. Therefore, I truly stay clear and far from my people like you.

So, let me close and slam my book and door in your face. Now you have and get the message that, I truly do not care for you, you're false, the Devil's Game; fame, and blame.

Michelle
September 18, 2021

Let no one tell you, War is the answer to life.
War is not the answer to life.

War is the answer for Death because, you have to stir up conflict,
and you have to; must kill.

Michelle
September 27, 2021

Those who are not of life cannot advocate for life,
nor can they advocate for peace or true peace.

They have to and must advocate for Death. Therefore, know the
difference between Life and Death.

Michelle
September 27, 2021

Life is the answer for life, and Death is the answer for Death.

Michelle
September 27, 2021

Life is not a battlefield but, many in life seek War and Strife over good and true life.

Michelle
September 27, 2021

Life isn't about Religion or confusion therefore, unconfuse you. Question the validity of all therefore, not all that glitters is gold.

Michelle
September 27, 2021

DREAMS

It's a new day Lovey. Good and Blessed Morning to you and me Lovey.

Wow to my dreams.

Russia – Vladimir Putin and his Filipino – Asian Looking Older Female Housekeeper.

I can't tell you the full extent of the dream as I cannot remember all of the dream.

See, Vladimir's housekeeper was a Spy.

This all had to do with a Code. A Code to what I do not know, but a Code, nonetheless.

Following Vladimir Putin, he went to this place. The maid – housekeeper was there.

I am pretty sure Vladimir Putin asked her if she was a Spy and she said no. He also said something to her pertaining to the Code and she repeated the Code.

I'm not sure why she repeated a Code that she should not know about. After repeating the Code, Vladimir Putin just took out a Gun and killed her just like that.

I am not sure if other people died because I now feared for my life – thought he was going to kill me.

No Lovey, this man, Vladimir Putin is heartless.

He's a cold-blooded Murder that is truly not afraid to kill at will.

Killing comes easy for this man.

No Lovey, how heartless can you be to kill just like that?

<u>Demons are heartless yes, but this Russian Demon surpass heartless.</u>

Lovey, People as heartless as Vladimir Putin, which part of Hell do these Monsters and or, Monsters like Vladimir Putin go?

Yes, I worry about him. Not Vladimir Putin but him, and I am going to leave it at that.

So now Lovey, which Asian, Southeast Asian, Indonesian Land is Spying on Russia and or, have Spies in Russia that Russian Officials do not know about for me to be seeing them?

<u>What is this Code Lovey, and what is Russia Developing under the quiet that the World truly do not know about?</u>

No Lovey, I will put nothing past the Russian President – Vladimir Putin.

<u>Threats are eliminated. But Lovey, how can you live for Death.</u>

<u>How can you be so heartless and cold; demonic?</u>

Wow, because I have to wonder if he literally drinks blood.

25

Wow

Allelujah

Wow

Yes, I know for Demons their Job is to get you to do ills here on Earth thus, locking you Physically and Spiritually in Hell.

But wow to the heartlessness of some humans thus, I see and many will class me a threat, dangerous to what I see them doing via my Dream World.

Michelle Jean
October 8, 2021
Edited October 09, 2021

Now Lovey. DAB wow.

Have not talked to him in years – over 2 years.

Called him in September, and recently in October.

He told me he took the Mark of the Beast – Vaccine.

I asked him when he was going to take me out before he told me he got Vaccinated.

I was my usual self with him.

He was to take me out the Week of October 17th but after hearing he took the Mark of the Beast that changed for me.

We caught up on the happenings of the past, and after; before we hung up, I told him I would call him next Month (November) if not the following Month.

Now, this morning I am dreaming about him. DAB

We were sitting on a bench outside with Green Grass.

Man, you could see the Fat Big Worms moving in the dirt – grass.

I said to him, you cut your hair. You didn't tell me you cut your hair. He said, no I believe.

DAB has dreadlocks in real life.

In the dream you could see his hair. He had no dreadlocks, and gray – this gray patch of hair in the Center and or, more to the front of his head.

Also, in the dream, his hair was going from not dreadlocks to dreadlocks; the beginning stage of growing dreadlocks and or, the growing stage of having dreadlocks.

Sitting there we didn't really talk, and because the Worms in the grass was getting bigger, I did not want any of the Worms to bite me and or, attach itself to my skin.

Now, my last child came outside, and I told him to get me my slippers so that I could put it on my feet.

He did, and I still did not feel comfortable with having sandals and or, slippers on.

Then, my son did the unthinkable. He picked up two short medium to chubby worms. One he threw at me I believe, and I warned him about doing that, and he stopped.

Now, one of the Worms — yellow, not too transparent, huge worm — think Fish like size and mouth came up and bit and or, almost bit DAB on his Fingernail.

DAB had to move his hand for the Worm not to bite him.

In the dream, he had to check his nail — fingernail again.

Yes, I know what this dream means.

Looking at the Grass, it glistened Yellow. Was truly beautiful, but the Huge Worms that was in it; the Grass was truly scary; not beautiful.

So yes, Lovey, the grass is truly not greener on the other side and or, with DAB.

The Crap of Worms.

Huge Worms inside the gras that come up from the Earth.

So yes, I will take my warning and heed your warning Lovey. I truly do not want or need to get mixed up in the Mess of Anyone.

Cannot take Bacchanal.

So yes, I will stay to myself – clean.

Clean must stay away from the unclean.

Michelle
October 8, 2021
Edited October 09, 2021

Now Lovey, this dream ties in with my DAB Dream in some way but why, I truly do not know.

Dreamt my niece and her son – last child.

Now someone – his mother was in Jamaica.

You know what, let me leave this dream alone because it's two families tied in one in the dream that turned out to be my daughter's sister's mother.

Darkness is around her; my daughter's sister's mother, and I am going to leave things as this because who feels it knows it.

Some women; Jamaican Women are nasty Negativity Wise. Therefore, it's not just Men alone that serve Death. Many women do also. Thus, many hath no soul to the evils they deal in.

Michelle
October 8, 2021

After writing and talking to you Lovey, thank you for answering me.

Lovey, Death cannot follow us on our journey.

I know the beginning will be hard, a tight squeeze, but I am trusting you Lovey for it not to be.

I know the Mode we must travel, therefore, be our good Mode of Transport always as, I am trusting you with our life Lovey.

Truly come through for us no matter the length of the journey and hardships.

So, thank you for my dream but, White People though.

Michelle
October 8, 2021

Oh lord Lovey. What now and again with Covid − 19 and the Chinese Race?

I dreamt I was in a Chinese Store that was selling Vaccines.

I did not take and or, buy the Vaccine but people were taking it, coming into the store to buy the Vaccine.

I saw one particular White Lady with Black Hair say in her fifties if not a tad younger.

I was talking to one of the Chinese Ladies that worked in the store.

I was telling her it is going to get worse, and she agreed.

I will not analyze this dream because I know the worst that is to come.

Michelle
October 8, 2021

No Lovey, humans have and has messed up life here on earth.

Humans did turn Earth – Mother Earth into the Realm of Death.

Humans did cause Death to infiltrate Earth – Mother Earth.

It is so bad here on Earth that I am sick and tired of the Global Mess; Slavery we are under right now due to their Covid – 19 bullshit.

No Lovey, why the hell can't these Leaders – Government Leaders and Pharmaceutical Greed be charged for Murder right now and they lose it all right now?

Yes, I am angry Lovey.

Do not take my rights to life from me. None of you are God; Lovey.

Michelle
October 8, 2021

Am I seeing faces before me?

Yes, but I cannot draw so therefore, I cannot draw the faces I see that are on the Docket of Death.

I am seeing Black Women. Older Black Women that I would say are in their Sixties that are going to die.

I see these people's faces as plain as day.

Some faces turn gross to the way they are going to die violently.

Sometimes it's not Death I see.

At times I will see ordinary people's face before me. They do not have a smile on their face. It's like their face is placid – yes, dead.

Was I seeing Elon Musk's face before me?

Yes

His face was placid. Had no smile.
His look looked dead – like a dead corpse to me.

Yes, I am thinking of him and his life. Not Elon Musk.

You know what, let me leave things alone because the things I see, many of you cannot see just like that.

Michelle
October 8, 2021

Was Mother Earth trying to show me something?

I am so not sure. It's as if she wants to tell me something but I was not able to receive her message.

<u>I am truly not sure if she was trying to show me this great destruction here on Earth but was not permitted to let me see.</u>

I know she will find a way to communicate her message to me somehow. Yes, it's troubling and worrying for me.

<u>Now Lovey, with Black People rejecting me; not accepting me. Please can you lead me truthfully to the people you want and need to save?</u>

I refuse to worry about the Black Race. I have no time for stupidity; their lying religious beliefs therefore, <u>BY-PASS BLACK PEOPLE PERIOD AND GO TO THE NEXT RACE TO BE SAVED ON OUR WELL, YOUR MOUNTAIN OF GOODNESS AND TRUTH.</u>

No Lovey, <u>NO ONE CAN TAKE LIES TO YOU,</u> AND I TRULY DO NOT KNOW WHY BLACK PEOPLE REFUSE TO LET GO OF LIES, AND START LIVING RIGHT – THE TRUTH.

<u>Slavery bound and or, bind the Black Race to Death, and I refuse to be like the Rest of the Black Race Period.</u>

35

No Lovey, IT GOES TO SHOW YOU THAT BLACK PEOPLE NEVER WANTED OR NEEDED GOOD AND TRUE LIFE FOR SELF. Therefore Lovey, leave the Black Race alone to their Death.

Literally completely walk away from all who truly do not want or need life. You cannot save any no matter the race or gender, ethnicity, sexual preference, colour of skin, and more. You Lovey cannot be trying with stiff-necked fools that cannot see their life, or add good and true value to their life come on now.

I need Life Lovey not Death.

The cost; value of 1 Sin is:

1, 152, 000 000 Years in Hell.

Why the hell would I want to go to hell and burn for this much time, and this cost does not include the days, months, and years I've Sinned for including, does not include the cost of my other sins?

No, Hell is truly not worth it.

Life – Good and True Life is better therefore, I have to; must hang on to Good and True Life come on now.

No Lovey, we do not have THE NEW BOOK OF KNOWLEDGE as written by Michelle & Lovey – God *for nothing come on now.*

Humans make life a battlefield hence, **HUMANS HAVE REPLACED GOD AND WITH THE SWORD.**

Michelle
October 8, 2021

It's raining outside and it's a new day. Walked Queenie and my countenance is so down this morning.

I cannot lash out at God this morning. All that is happening here on Earth is truly not God's fault. The fault is on humans.

It is us as humans that gave birth to demons. Demons that live to kill, hath not life's worth or truth.

Some leaders have no backbone or spine because they bow to the needs of the United States of Death; America. __They could care less for their citizens because they are a joke.__

I truly do not know how some women lay with these Weak and Kiss Ass Men, no not men; toys for those who own them; the United States of Death; America.

What the hell Lovey, we are not Americans; of the United States of Death; America so, why is this world and or, the people of this world; Earth shaped by the iniquities of Death; them; the United States of Death; America?

No Lovey, let me calm my temper because all that is happening here on Earth is truly not right. No, I am getting pissed, but then; __MEN'S LAWS ARE INCORRECT; LIES TOLD ON YOU BY THEM WHO WROTE THE BOOK OF DEATH; THEIR SO-CALLED HOLY BIBLE SO, I SHOULD EXPECT NOTHING LESS FROM THE DEMONS THAT CONTROL AND RUN THE CORPORATIONS OF THE WORLD.__

__DEMONS THAT THINK IN ALL THEY ARE DOING THEY CONTROL IT ALL BUT A PITY__

NONE KNOW(S) THE HELL THAT THEY MUST AND ARE GOING TO FACE ONCE THEIR SPIRIT SHED THE FLESH. AND IT MATTERS NOT LOVEY IF THEY ARE CREMATED. THE BURNING OF FLESH AND BONES IS TRULY NOT THE BURNING OF THEIR SPIRIT. *So, no, I worry not about the Wicked and Evil of this World and the Wicked and Evil People that run the different corporations of Death and Dishonesty. My concern is the unjust laws they are imposing on people to let people bow down to their bully tactics.*

Where is my life here on Earth Lovey and Mother Earth?

No Mother Earth I am getting pissed at you because you allow demons to take all from you at will.

This is bullshit. Where are the Laws of Earth Mother Earth?

Where the hell are your Laws that shut these demons that control the Global Marketplace down?

Where is my right to life in you Mother Earth to live Debt and Death Free?

No, because I want to lash out at you real Nasty now Mother Earth.

No, I want you to get pissed.

Why the hell is Corporate Greed and Governmental Greed – Demonic Leaders not fighting for my rights?

Why are Whites implementing unjust laws for humans to live by globally via the stinking dutty demented leaders of the globe.

No BC man now.

F, F, F, F, F.

Yes, Mother Earth, I would like to say boldly to you, F You because you are weak; spineless when it comes to protecting the good and true of life, but I cannot do that. I have to leave you alone and respect the decision you make to house, strengthen, maintain, and sustain Evil.

Just as Man humans are unjust, you Mother Earth have to be unjust also. I truly hate to say it, but this is the way I feel right now. I refuse to lie to you when it comes to my anger and feel.

Nothing is going right right now in you Mother Earth.

It's like I want to give up hope in you that you can make a major change for the good and true. For me, and to me, you truly do not care about me and the good and true that still reside in you.

How can you let Evil People – Demons control you like that Mother Earth?

How can you allow all…you know what, let me forget it because right now Mama; Mother Earth, I am truly disappointed in you.

Evil's time is up.

Wicked and Evil People – Humans and Spirit should not be gaining in you come on now.

WHERE ARE THE LAWS OF LIFE AND GOD IN YOU MAMA; MOTHER EARTH?

Mi belly

Mi belly Mother Earth.

DOES GOD NOT MATTER TO YOU?

DO I NOT MATTER TO YOU?

THE CHILDREN AND PEOPLE OF LIFE, DO THEY NOT MATTER TO YOU?

WHERE IS YOUR LOYALTY TO GOOD AND TRUE LIFE MOTHER EARTH?

DOES ANYTHING MATTER TO YOU ANYMORE CONSIDERING HUMANS RAPE AND ABUSE YOU DAILY?

NO, YOU'VE BECOME POWERLESS AND A VICTIM DUE TO NEGATIVITY; ALL THE EVILS THAT RESIDE IN YOU.

Yes, sad but reality because, **we both know just how hard it is to get rid of evil from within, and outer.**

THIS IS LOVE by Monsta feat. J. Boog

Truly thank you Mother Earth.

Truly thank you. I need you. I cannot do without you.

Good, true, and real love all the time Mama; Mother Earth.

You are a true part of my life and world.

Michelle
October 9, 2021

Injustice is truly not Justice Mother Earth come on now.

Life is truly not death Mother Earth.

Right now, I am at a loss because I truly do not know what to do for you Mother Earth, Lovey, the Universe, all my good and true guides, and Death to hear me.

I guess I have to leave things alone and trust in all of you to work things out for the best of the Good and True Children and People of Earth that has not fallen prey to the Mark of the Beast, Unjust Corporations, and Political Leaders that feel the need to rape and massacre humans of their Fundamental Human Rights, and Human Rights.

Yes, Hell but right now, Hell cannot soothe my pain, the pain I am feeling right now.

As for my dreams I am going to leave them alone because they truly do not make any sense to me.

My dreams right now cannot help me. Black Men need a true wake up call. Many live for Sexual Pleasure and this is truly not right.

And I am not going to get involved in this Mother Earth and Lovey. Right now, Sexual Gratification of Black Men and Women is truly not my concern.

My concern is my life and the life of the Children and People of Life.

I am fretting therefore, I have to come to You Mother Earth and Lovey for strength, true hope, true victory over our enemies.

I am weak strength wise right now.

I need your strength in a good way right now.

As a Child of you both, Mother Earth and You Lovey, I have to come to you. Tell you both the truth of my struggles and lack of hope right now.

For me, and to me, evil should not be gaining and winning. Evil; all Evil should be shutting down and I do not see it.

The Governments of the Globe are not quaking in their boots of their penalties in our book THE NEW BOOK OF KNOWLEDGE LOVEY COME ON NOW.

Come on Lovey, humans are Flesh and Spirit. Once the Spirit shed the Flesh then comes the Judgement for some. And yes, Life for those who are a true part of life.

Michelle
October 9, 2021

BOOKS WRITTEN BY MICHELLE JEAN 2021

MY TALK JANUARY 2021

MY TALK JANUARY 2021 – BOOK TWO

MINI BOOK

JUST TALKING – THINKING

A LITTLE TALK WITH MOTHER EARTH

I NEED ANSWERS GOD

POETRY MY WAY

THE MIND AND SPIRITUALITY

I NEED ANSWERS GOD – PART TWO

MY NIGHTS

I NEED ANSWERS GOD – PART THREE

GOD IS GOOD

WHAT ABOUT US

WOW WHAT

AFRICAN – BLACK PEOPLE CUSS OUT

THE FIFTH WAVE – BLACK PEOPLE WARNING

FINAL CALL

JUST MY TALK 2021

THE TRAP

CHANGES

RACIST OR NOT

GIVE ME A REASON – SPIRITUAL CLEANSING

LIFE AFTER DEATH

THE DAYS LIFE SUCKS

MOVING UP – MY HEART TO HEART WITH LOVEY – GOD 2021

DAY BY DAY

THE MARK OF THE BEAST CLARIFIED

I REFUSE

COMING SOON
THE HARDSHIPS OF WALKING WITH GOD

THE HARDSHIPS OF WALKING WITH GOD is not a hard book to write, but it's not time for this book. I so do not know if God want or need me to continue to write this book.

Hopefully, I will get to write this book. As for other books, I truly do not know what the next one will be. So, you might have a random book as I truly do not know the name of my next book other than THE HARDSHIPS OF WALKING WITH GOD.

Michelle